Dedication

To my precious wife, Chrissie thank you so much for all your help and kindness.

To Whiskers (Wikkie) you give me so much joy.

Bernard Levine

HOW TO FIND A JOB QUICKLY AND EASILY
By Bernard Levine

Let me start off by saying, that I know that this book is going to be highly controversial and people will be shocked by the methods and techniques which I provide to help and enable someone to get a job.

Because the ways spoken about in this unique book are not the everyday norm (how the mass and every Tom, Dick and Harry goes about getting a job) ....your first response will probably be that the ideas expressed in this book are wrong and will not work...but before you attack, criticise and condemn, hold onto your horses! I'm telling you, that although the ways will all seem strange and perhaps even bizarre, never mind, I am not writing this book to please the Employment Personnel Agencies, and this book is not going to appeal to the staff who are working in Human Resources in gigantic Corporations...this book is aimed at the unemployed who are sick and tired of being rejected time and time again...having their CV's thrown into File 13 without ever getting any feedback, response to their job applications leaving them angry, frustrated and depressed.

But that's exactly why it does work because instead of you doing what everybody else does and standing in a long row trying to get them to notice and accept you....this book will show you how you are going to stand out from the rest...how you will make a big impression and how your interview and you yourself will be well remembered.

So, we are going to try something different ....we are going on a very different route to find and secure a job.

I'm not interested in what others who are smug in their well paid jobs have to say, nor do I care.

I'm going to go out of my way to give people hope, using a little imagination and igniting the sparks of greatness that lead to a path of success and victory.

Thinking of You

I am thinking of you today
and I want you to know
that no matter what your situation is
God's help is so mighty
Keep your eyes on His awesome power
and your heart focused on His never-ending love
Ask God to open the door that is closed
to make the way clear for you
His strength is beyond our understanding
His ways are so miraculous and complete
God deeply loves you
And your victory is just around the corner!

Always Have a Dream

Follow your heart
to the path of greatness
that lies within you.

The secret of life
is to have something
to look forward to
everyday.

Find a dream that excites you
and make plans
of how you are going
to achieve it.

Feed your mind daily
with positive energy
and words of inspiration.

Take your life to a higher level.
Stay focused and go forward
with your eyes on the prize.

**When you run towards your destination
with passion in your heart
you will see your dreams come true.**

Dear Reader

I want you to know, that I am passionate and determined to see that you get a job and find it quickly and urgently!

And for you to find a job, you must always remember...

getting a job is just a numbers game...that's what it is!

I repeat, and cannot stress enough that the way you are going to find a job will be a numbers game.

Let me explain and illustrate what I mean and how it really will be by telling you a true story.

This tale I am about to tell you, is the working principle of how getting a job really is and has become.

With our huge population, there are lots of mice out there that are all chasing the same block of cheese.

Because the availability of these jobs are sometimes very limited, with so many candidates all applying for the same job, the secret is you have to stand out from the pack and be head and shoulders way above the rest.

This story might shock you, but that is part of my plan. You see the reason I am going to tell you this story, is that I want the message of the story to stick and stay in your mind...I want you to know that the truth you will discover in this story, will be like finding a job.

Here is what really happened....

You see, there is this guy, let's call him Abe....he wakes up in the morning with a dreadful unbearable pain inside.

Abe goes to the Doctor who examines him and tells him: 'Abe, it breaks my heart to tell you this news....

Abe, you have an incurable disease and only have 3 days on average to live.

I'm sorry I can't help you. You've lived a fairly long life...how old are you now?'

Abe answered: 'I'm 88'.

The Doctor responded: 'Is there anything that you regret in your life that you were not able to do? ...or shall I say, that you wanted to do, but never got around to doing it?'

Abe replied: 'Yes, Doctor there is this one thing....

I've never kissed a woman?'

The Doctor's face showed his surprise: 'How come you have never been able to do this?'

Abe added: 'You see Doctor...I'm very short, I have pimples on my face and as you know, I stutter ...

and because of all this, women find me very unattractive!'

The Doctor smiled and said: 'Abe, I know a way that you will definitely have your wish come true....here's how you will get the success you are looking for....

All you've got to do is on a Saturday morning, go visit a busy Shopping Mall, go early...be there just before the shops open and stand outside a busy store and every woman you see that passes by, you say to her:

'Hi, my name is Abe...I want to kiss you!' Even if she is holding a man's hand, it doesn't matter, you just carry on telling every woman that you see 'My name is Abe...I want to kiss you! What have you got to lose?'

Abe could hardly believe his ears what his trusted Doctor had just told him...Abe wanted to be absolutely sure and asked: 'Will it work Doctor?'

The Doctor answered: 'The law of averages will never let you down! It's a numbers game. All of your 88 years you have not succeeded in knowing how it feels to kiss a woman...now I'm telling you, if you want to see results this will definitely work...it's a guaranteed method!   Take it from me and just go do what I told you to do....If you don't try, you will never know! It's Saturday tomorrow, so why don't you choose a busy Shopping Centre, be positive and the results will come!'

So Abe went along to Sandon Shopping Mall and he stood outside Woolworths.

The first woman strolled past...

'Hi! My name is Abe. I want to kiss you?'

'X@y&*z,' You Pig!!! she walked away totally disgusted.

The second woman that Abe saw and approached, spat in his face.

The third woman's response was to hit him in the eye!

But the Doctor told Abe not to stop but to just carry on regardless.

At 5 o'clock, the Doctor arrived at the Shopping Mall to see how Abe was getting on.

'Look at me Doctor! I have a black eye, I have been sworn at, kicked and spat upon! Your method doesn't work!'

The Doctor was astonished and taken aback: 'I'm really terribly sorry Abe...I can't understand why it did not work...I mean how many women did you ask? How many women walked past?'

'There was at least a hundred that walked by that I approached and asked' Abe sadly replied.

'Well Abe! It should have worked! I tell you what, you must be very hungry....sit down and relax while I go get you a cheese burger, some chips and a coke...I won't be long!'.

After fifteen minutes, the Doctor returned with the food and drink but Abe was no where to be found.

The Doctor then phoned Abe 'I've got the food...where are you? '

Abe laughed 'You see Doctor, I decided to just carry on talking to the ladies....and when you left, this woman walks past and I called out 'My name is Abe...I want to kiss you!'

She replied: 'Yes, certainly! I would like to kiss you too! Shall we go to your place or mine?'

'I'm now at her home and we are getting to know each other!'

If you think about it, the principle, the success and the results of finding a job are exactly the same as this story.

How can you expect to find a job if you only approach one company? You might be lucky, but I'm not talking about luck! I'm talking about maximizing your chances and increasing the possibilities of actually securing a job offer.

The more companies you try, the more opportunities and chances of success you will have.

Here's what I want you to do....

Get hold of your local area Yellow Pages (or find the 'Yellow Pages' on the web or at your nearest library)

Start going through the Yellow Pages phone book looking at the many different categories where businesses, companies and services are advertised.... for example... you will find...Accounting Software, Stationery Manufacturers, Motor Vehicle Spares, Fibreglass Moulding, Pharmaceutical Companies....and so on.

Make a list of the companies where you would like to work, taking note of the physical address where they are situated.

How far would you have to travel to get to work?

If possible, you don't want to have to travel too far to get to and from work every day...so choose wisely companies situated in areas close to your home.

Now, get a notepad and pen and write down your list of at least 20 companies in areas close to your home, where you would like to work.

Next, make a list of all the different kinds of jobs that you are able to do....or the specific jobs that you would like to do at the companies which you have just listed.

Remember, that if you only put down one type of work that you are willing to perform or do at a company, then you are cutting short and limiting your chances of success.

Here's what I mean....

If you only look for Business Analyst jobs, what will you do if there are only 6 companies where you can apply to be a Business Analyst and they all turn you down? Then you have nothing and you are back to square one!

You have to have a second or third choice of the type of work that you are able to perform at a company. You have to have a backup plan.

So, on the first page of your notebook make a list of ALL the various and different type of jobs you have the knowledge of and can actually do at any given company.

Here's an example….

If you want to get into sales, but the company offered you a job in telemarketing would you accept?

So now, instead of having just one position you can apply for….you have now got two different posts you can apply for instead of just one…you are creating more opportunities for yourself either being a Sales Consultant or you can also be a Telemarketer.

Would you be able to do demonstrations of products for the company?...then they could offer you a job doing promotions and demonstrations, perhaps even arranging events, sales meetings, business networking and functions, sending out invitations to buyers and clients, following up and co-ordinating the whole launch and its activities.

Could you do cold calling, like gathering information and doing research, providing leads and making sales appointments for the Consultants?

If you are able to do this, then you could become a Canvasser, a New Business Manager or work in Marketing.

Are you able to handle queries from the public, listen to their complements or complaints? ...there could be good opportunities waiting for you being in Customer Care or Reception.

I want you to prepare and think about the wording of the email you are going to send out to get that job interview.

You have to send out lots and lots of emails to get a job interview.

The more email letters you send, the greater will be your chances of having several job interviews.

So, set yourself a goal to send out at least one email letter every day to a company.

If you send just one email every day, then by the end of the month you will have sent 30 emails.

Let's expect a positive reply of 10%...so we are talking about having 3 companies who will contact you and ask you to come in for an interview.

Here is an email idea you can use:

Dear Warren Smith

I would like to work at XYZ to provide you with new clients for Microsoft Dynamics CRM.

<u>You might want to tell them how you are going to do this....</u>

Here's what I will do to bring in more clients...(who will be interested in buying your products or the service that you offer):

Or

Here is how I will bring in the new software clients:

I will be phoning the key decision makers at companies doing research on the current accounting software they are using.

I will be recording this information into an Accounting Software Database with categories like:

What is the name of the accounting software they are using?

Which version do they have?

How many users are there?

Which modules have they got?

What problems are they having?

From the leads I have generated, I will be setting up appointments for the sales consultants to meet the new clients.

New doors are going to open for XYZ as we go forward to reach new heights and break new sales records.

I look forward to hearing from you.

Warm Regards

Bernard Levine

Or perhaps you would like to send an email that is short and sweet...to the point!

I would like to work at Woodlands

Dear Madam / Sir

I would like to work at Woodlands as a Telemarketer.

Here's what I would like to do at your company:

I would like to fill your diaries with lots of qualified accounting sales appointments.

Or

I would like to provide you with more clients and increase your sales turnover.

I look forward to hearing from you.

Warm Regards

Bernard Levine

Where would you be without any income at all? You don't want to go down that route at all!

Half a loaf is better than no bread at all!

Yes, there are times that you have to lower your salary expectations and take whatever salary you get offered.

...at least, even if the salary they offer is way below what you really want, this low salary, although not to your liking will still be much better than at the end of the month having no income at all to bring home.

I know that by taking a lower salary you might not be able to meet all your monthly commitments and responsibilities, but the money you receive could just be the difference between survival mode and being utterly destitute.

One of the most important things to consider is you might not like doing the job they are offering you, but for the meantime you've got to put food on the table and be able to live.

If you can't find the job you actually want and like, instead of just declining that job offer and sitting at home doing nothing, take the work they give you and use the opportunity you have to add to your experience ….and then while you are at the company earning an income, you will be able to look around until you can find something better, more to your liking with a better salary than you are now receiving.

You've got to persevere….you must not give up.

If you get rejected, so what! There are plenty fish out in the sea…as the song goes…it's all about picking yourself up, dusting yourself off and starting all over again!

How to get Job interviews

It's a connections game….Who are your connections?

It's not what you know...it's who you know.

You've got to reach out and spread your wings to meet new contacts....you've got to widen your circle of contacts.

Try joining Networking Groups, or go attend business breakfasts...also make a list of friends, neighbours, family members who could introduce you to their business contacts and connections.

Make a list of 100 people you know or influential contacts.

Who's your hairdresser?...and your doctor and dentist?

Who are your children's teachers?

Who lives across the road from you?

Who do you know at your church?

Who goes to the same Gym as you?

What's the name of the owner or manager of your local supermarket?

What's the name of your Vet?

Who services your car?

Very soon you will see your list of contacts expanding greatly and very soon you will have your Top 100 names who could perhaps help you or tell you who to contact using their name as a referral.

How do most people go about getting a job?

Everybody is doing the same thing!

They all just post their CV on several job websites, or they go for interviews and leave their CV at a number of Employment Personnel Agencies hoping for the best! ...and most times, that's where it stays and nothing happens!

Many of the staff working in Human Resources Departments or at Personnel Agencies just don't care. They treat you like a number and as soon as you leave their office, your file is placed right at the bottom of the pile or stored away in the draw and then they attend to the next in line job candidate...'Next please!'

You've got to stand out from the rest of the pack.

You've got to make your mark and be remembered!

How do you do this?

I don't believe that you should just talk and carry on talking at your interview.

It is very boring hearing someone rambling on and on.

Go buy yourself a flip-file….it's a file that has lots of see-through plastic sleeves.

What you are going to do is 'Show & Tell'!

One of the big secrets of success is preparation!

The more you prepare, the luckier you will get!

This 'Show & Tell' file is going to be your 'Achievement File' for your prospective Employer to get to know you better.

If you have any copies of Diplomas or Degrees, put them inside the plastic sleeves of this file.

If you are married, insert a photo of your partner into one of the sleeves in the file.

Let your future Employer get to know you…much more than your CV can say, let them see your life story in pictures.

Because every picture tells a story and one picture is worth more than a thousand words.

Show them a photo of your house.. that is only if you feel it will leave a good impression…otherwise don't have this photo in your file.

Place a copy of your ID Document in the file.

Do you have any newspaper clippings about yourself?…School or sporting achievements etc

Are you a member of any professional organization, or club memberships...you might like to show them these photos or certificates.

To have greater visual impact, only use colour photo copies in your file.

It's all about likeability and trust.

You've got to make them like you and trust you.

They've got to feel comfortable in your company.

You've got to make them want you by telling them what you can offer....what you are able to do at the company.

Please set yourself a goal to contact at least 3 companies every day.

After you have contacted, and gone personally to meet the decision makers at between 20 and 30 companies, clearly identifying what you are able to do for them, you will find that the odds will be very much in your favour for you to have several job proposals that you will be able to choose from.

When you call, give them an alternative:

Would you prefer seeing me in the beginning of the week or the latter part of the week?

Would you prefer a morning appointment or an afternoon appointment?

God Cares Deeply About You

Whatever trouble you might be facing in your life
Whatever storm clouds are on the horizon
Whatever roadblocks are standing in your way
God cares deeply about you.
If you're looking for true victory in your life
then give your love to Jesus
Faster than lightening can strike
and quicker than a wheel can turn
God will move in a miraculous way
to create wonderful miracles for you!

Have you considered working for yourself?

Sometimes the job market and the circumstances surrounding the job market are not favourable and even after you have tried and tried, you still may not have succeeded in finding a job.

With your priority and main purpose of urgently needing to get a regular monthly income to provide for your daily living expenses and necessities, the right solution might be for you to start your own business.

But you may ask, how can I start my own business without having any money?

There are a number of businesses you can start with either having no money at all or with a minimal cash outlay.

Let's look at some of the businesses you can start:

Can you cut hair? ....start your own men's hairdressing salon from your home.

A garden service...somebody I know took his lawnmower, spade, fork and rake and went door-to-door to homes in his neighbourhood.

And today...he sits at home answering the phone for his garden service business, while his team of 12 drivers with their gardeners are busy cleaning up company gardens.

Baby sitting service

Home tutoring providing extra lessons in maths, science, language lessons to name a few subjects you might consider doing.

School shuttle service....fetching and taking children to school, ballet, karate, swimming lessons, etc

Care giver....providing a service to retirement villages and old age homes taking the residents to shopping centres, doctor's appointments, hairdressers ...

Small parcel and letter delivery service

Selling garden pot plants to businesses

Cooking and baking classes

Looking after pets

Entertaining at children's parties

Having a flea market stall for the crafts you make

Dress making and tailoring

Using your voice, narrating

Translating from one language to another

Teaching magic to children

Teaching pupils how to play a musical instrument like guitar, piano or singing lessons

Homework supervision

Teaching people to draw or paint...art classes

Massage and reflexology

Painting owner's homes

House cleaning service especially new homes before the buyers take occupation

Start your own Estate Agency sales and rentals

Have your own community newspaper

Pool cleaning

Carpentry and home improvements

Making Signs

Printing

Wedding planner

Spring cleaning service

Car valet

Photography especially attending sporting events at schools and also school photography

Wedding photography

Company news letters

Pet grooming

Antique and Collectibles Dealer

Book and Magazine Dealer

Apartment Locator

Debt Collection Agency

Computer Tutor for Children

Online copywriter

Correspondence Club

Dating and Escort Service

Directory Publisher

Employment Agency

Errand Service

Gift Basket Business

Magic at children's birthday parties

Food Delivery Service

Freelance Photographer

Freelance Writer

Make your own greeting cards for sale

Babysitting and day care

Baking/cooking start an online shop

Photography lessons

Web programming

Computer repair

Social media consulting

Fitness instruction

Write slogans for companies

Life coaching

Beauty consultations

Clean homes

Invitation printing

Matchmaker service

Print merit and award certificates

Newsletter publishing

Newspaper clipping service

Personalized stationery

Photography family portraits, animals, children, events

Make custom wooden furniture

Sell advertising

Bookkeeping

Yoga Facilitator

Teach dance classes

Make and sell baby blankets

Sell handmade jewellery

Printing Broker

Printer toner recharging

Personalised invitations

Proof-reader

Real estate magazine

Real Estate Agent

Sell bottled water at events

Reporter

Rubber stamps for businesses

Voice over artist

Apartment preparation service

Telemarketing

Using your car or van to make money

Sell flower arrangements

Start an office cleaning company

Home cleaning

Make your own sauces and sell at flea markets

Make and sell birdhouses and bird feeders

Make scratch boards and tunnels for cats

Last minute accommodation

Writing press releases

Start a list of Properties to rent in your area

Start an area newspaper and sell advertising

Sell plastic, cardboard, newspapers, metal, bottles, cans

Sell celebrity autographed photos (which you get for free) to restaurants and interior decorators.

See 'Make money collecting books, get free celebrity autographs and more!' by Bernard Levine

ISBN-13: 978-1502850164

Baby sitting service

Sell your own bottled pickles and cultured foods

List of holiday homes to rent

Put poetry onto trays, mirrors

Print or make and sell car-signs

Taxi Service for seniors, children and everyone

Look for car manuals to sell

Sell second hand toys

Sell sheet music manuscripts

Paint and sell pine cones as Christmas decorations

Find sterling silver at charity shops and sell on Ebay

Look for vintage watches to sell

Sell porcelain

Vinyl records sell on Ebay

Sell corporate gifts

Make money collecting and selling

See 'Make money collecting everyday easy to find items' by Bernard Levine

ISBN-13: 978-1503172036

100's of Opportunities
for you to make money

BERNARD LEVINE

'100's of Opportunities for you to make money'
by Bernard Levine

ISBN-13: 978-1515044413

Advertise your own business on websites where you
don't have to pay, make signs to put up on notice
boards or free advertising in your local community
newspapers...put signs up at the public library,
restaurants, take-away outlets, the church notice

board and where ever there is a constant flow of people who will see your posters.

Search and go through all your belongings in your cupboards. See what you have that you don't want or don't use any more, items that you can sell that will bring in quick cash.

And most important of all...please don't forget to pray!

Very often, we try too hard in our own strength.

You've got to 'let go and let God' take over your life.

Ask God to open doors and lead you to the right opportunities and bring the right people into your life.

It's Your Time for a Mighty Breakthrough

Things might look impossible to you
but God's power is greater than you can imagine
God has no limits
God will do more for you
than you could ever ask or think

No person or obstacle can stand against God

It's not up to the world to decide on your success

It's up to God

Don't give up on your faith

Don't be discouraged

Keep believing and going forward

Keep your eyes on the prize

You don't know the wonderful things

God has waiting for you around the corner

God will bring the right people to cross your path

God will take you to a new higher level

Let God's Word repair your hurt and self-image

Make God your best friend

Praise God with your whole heart

and you will see how much God will richly reward you.

PRAYER

There is no greater joy

than loving God in prayer

There are no riches more rewarding

than the eternal treasures you'll receive

Prayer brings powerful help into your life
Prayer changes circumstances
What a wonderful privilege we have
to give our heart to our Father in prayer.

Look to Jesus for Your Victory

When your heart is broken
When your world is tumbling down
Whatever you are going through
I want you to know
God will deliver you
and everything is going to be all right
Your path may seem unclear right now
but soon you will see
that God's mighty power
will let you have your victory
So praise Him in the storm
Praise Him in the trial

Live one day at a time
and the miracle you so long for
will suddenly come to be!

There's a new world just around the corner waiting to unfold especially for you.

There are lots of wonderful gifts, miracles and wonders coming your way but nothing will happen until you make it happen.

Happiness and success are what you make happen for yourself!

You Hold the Key

Let your determination
be so strong that nothing
can sway its course.
Let your mind believe
so intensely that your dreams
become reality.
Let your actions be rich
with enthusiasm that it moves
the hearts of all.
Let your life be filled

with greater purpose
To reach Higher
To think bigger
To love deeper
than you've ever done before!

The Magic in You

Keep your eyes on the stars
and the stars in your eyes
Make the most of every precious moment
Remember - every breath is a miracle
and every day is a gift
You were made with a rare uniqueness
to fulfil a special purpose
Reward yourself
with the very special things you like
Never under-estimate the power
of a seed of love
planted into another's life

Send someone a signal
that they really matter
Follow your heart's secret desires
and you will find your magic rainbow
Never give up on your dreams!

Advice for your Job Interview

Start your day with a good positive attitude.

Dress for success.... always dress formally portraying a professional image.

Before going to a job interview, the best you can do is prepare and anticipate some answers to the questions they might ask you.

'Tell me about yourself.'

Give them only positive feedback...don't complain and moan...all the bad things that have happened to you in the past is not their business, and besides they are not really interested.

Think why you are there?

You've come to get a job...you have to impress and convince them...you are not there to tell them about your problems. They are looking for positive people who can contribute and be an asset to the company...what they are not looking for is misery and a 'woe is me' attitude.

Leave your problems at home...don't bring it to your job interview.

Tell them about your best achievements and personal attributes.

'Why do you want to work at our company?'

Make sure you do research on each company on the internet prior to visiting them.

And before going for your interview, you must prepare how you are going to answer this question if it comes up.

You might want to tell them that you see their company as being a market leader and you think highly of them.

Try to arrive at your interview at least 10 minutes before your appointment.

Put a smile on your face.

Impress the recruiter with your skills

Don't take your friends, family or one of your parents along to the interview ...this might leave the impression that you are insecure and cannot make decisions for yourself.

Switch off your cell phone before the interview. If your phone rings, this will interrupt the proceedings of your interview and may spoil your chances of getting a job.

Avoid all negative conversation...let your speech be positive displaying a good attitude.

Be friendly and warm.

You've got to set the vibe...you've got to create the right mood, the right atmosphere.

Be confident and remain positive.

If they sense from the way you carry yourself that you are worried, or tense ....this does not leave them with a good impression and it won't encourage them to present you with a job offer.

Believe in yourself and believe in the power of God.

God Is Your Partner

All David had was just 5 stones and a sling

and God gave him the victory

All the boy had was only 5 loaves and 2 fishes

and God used this to feed 5000

All Moses could speak was with a stuttering tongue

and God chose him to free his people

God can use

whatever you may

have

When you pray with all your heart

your prayers become miracles

When you sow seeds of praise

your love for God will be greatly rewarded

When you make God your priority

your life will have deep fulfilment.

Dear Friend

I just had to write this to you….

I've just got to tell you something important….

I know things for you haven't been easy…you've been through a lot….you've been deeply hurt….your pain is intense ….you've been wondering why your life has been through so much trouble….so much frustration…so many tests, trials and hardship.

You've been let down ….you've been disappointed time and time again….you've given up hope and just don't care anymore….

I just want to tell you that in all this….God is here

God has seen every tear that you have cried….God has felt your pain and knows what you are going through…God really wants to help you ….He is there….but you have to first turn the key….you have to open the door wide.

When a heart is broken….when a life is in ruin….it's not easy to pick up the pieces and start all over again….but you have to!….there's no other way up!….you have to let go!….it's a brand new season….it's the start of a new day....I know you just can't forget what has happened...... but you have to make a new life for yourself....you have to get out of the river and walk over to the mountain....there is help ....and there is hope.

The Hand of God

Things are now going to change for you....life is going to start getting better....you're now on your way to a new beginning....tell me, what do you want out of life?....what are your deepest dreams that you want to see come true?.....what is very important to you?.....what do you value the most?

Life isn't just a straight line....it's got curves, bends, ups and downs....you've had a lot of down-time for too long now.....it's now time for you to rise up....you know all the beauty that once was in your heart....it can still be found if you search deep within....you know what's true and you know your feelings...the dreams and wishes you have that you want to see come true....but how is this all going to happen for you?....how do you make a lemon into a lemonade?....how do you find the way to a more richer fulfilment?

THE POWER OF ALMIGHTY GOD

Please don't look to man for the answers....you will be disappointed....please don't try to find the solution all by yourself....our ways are so limited and we are very fragile and weak....but there is a God who is here with almighty power, and all the know-how in the world, together with all the ability, divine intervention and strength to change each and everything in your life all for the better.

If God could make water come out of a rock for Moses....then it's easy for God to make a miracle in your life all in an instant. If God could create a man out of just dust....then surely God can bring about exciting wonderful changes in your life.

You are a child of God

What do you have to do to see your miracle take place? What should you do to start a new life?....to make things better?.... to bring blessings, gifts and wonders come your way? All you've got to do is ask God?....but maybe you already have done this and nothing has happened....why did your requests not come to pass?....did you ask God for greed or for need?

The wisdom of Solomon

Let's look at King Solomon... what did he ask God for?.....he didn't ask for things of this world like a mansion, palace or castle filled with lots of gold and treasure .....all Solomon asked God for was for wisdom .....but God looked at his heart and saw that his heart was pure....God gave him knowledge and wisdom together with understanding ....because Solomon didn't look for self-gain and did not ask for worldly greed but Solomon asked for spiritual blessings and needs....God was so moved by Solomon's request that God gave him wisdom plus on top of that, God enriched his life with treasure in such great abundance!

The Greatest Power in the World

When you come to God you are coming to a King....not just any King....but the King of the Universe, Creator of everything. Yes, God is your Father and you are His beloved child, but God is holy, upright and pure...God is so beautiful ....our minds just cannot conceive, think or imagine how magnificent, how glorious, how amazing and how brilliant is our God....there are no words which we know that can describe God's loveliness, His awesomeness, His splendour!

Before you look at your needs and all the things that you want from God.....let's look at what God wants from us.

What is God looking for? What pleases God?....God wants recognition...God wants acceptance....God wants our appreciation....God wants our love....God wants a relationship with us....God wants us to get to know Him....but How?

By reading and studying God's Word we find out what God likes.... Tell God you love Him...let God know that there is nothing in your life more vital, more necessary or more important than Him!

Even the little things

Don't take God for granted…thank God for even the little things….did you ever say thank you to God for water?....where would we be without water? …..thank God for the streams, rivers, waterfalls, the oceans, the springs and the rain ….how about saying thank you to God for sand?....that's right, I'm being serious, without the soil, the earth….without the ground ….we won't have food….there would not be vegetables or fruit ….nor flowers, nor trees and grass!

Don't come to God every day with the same boring prayer!....get yourself a book and write down the things that you need to say 'thank you' to God for….you've got to move God's heart….you've got to touch God by showing Him that you are grateful for even the tiny little things in your life.

Thank God for the gift of air….for the breath of life….thank God that He has given mankind the ability to think and create inventions to make our lives easier and more enjoyable…inventions like the fridge, the computer, electricity. God just doesn't want lip service….you must truly believe and feel it in your heart for what you are thanking Him for.

Don't be lazy and just say 'thank you God for everything'…..No! You must be specific!....you must tell God which blessings, gifts or miracles you are grateful for.

Why is it so important to say thank you to God?

Imagine that you are a child and on Monday you come to your father and ask him for money for clothing….without hesitation, he gives this to you….then on Tuesday, you come again and ask for more money to go out and have a good time with your friends….and again he lovingly gives this to you….and a few days later, you ask your father again for something that you want….How does your father feel? ….every time you ask for something, but he never hears you say 'thank you'….your father begins to feel that you are always demanding more and more without showing appreciation.

It's the same with God…He is our Father and we are His children….God is not a shopping mall or a money bank….you can't just come to Him and expect Him to give you what you want without ever thanking Him for all the many, exceptional and wonderful gifts and blessings He has already given you….Thank you God that I can walk, stand, sit….thank you God for sleep, for rest, for peace…Thank you God for the beautiful gift of colours….for the stars….for the seasons….for the gift of music…for all the different types and varieties of flowers….for herbs and vitamins….Thank you Father God for Jesus….

Every day, take time to thank God for different specific gifts and blessings in your life …..for things that you have never thanked Him for before.

Start a 'I'm grateful for list'.... Look at all the amazing wonders of nature....marvel at the miracle of your brain....the precious gift of your eyes....your living skin.

Your life will have a deep inner fulfilment and take on a new meaning....you will realize that God is truly good and God wants to bless you more and more....and when you show God that you do not take Him for granted and all that He has already given you....all that He has already done....like all the times He has protected you....and for all the days He has loved you ....for His patience...for His forgiveness and grace....

When you show God that you are grateful even for the small things in your life....when your heart is filled with appreciation and praise, you will always be rewarded with mighty miracles.

You have the power of choice and the gift of prayer to change the circumstances and situations in your life....when God looks at your heart, will He see gratitude?

SHOW YOUR LOVE TO GOD

To God Be The Glory

To have a deep hunger for God

and love Him as much as we can

To delight ourselves in the study of His Word

To put Jesus first in our lives

and worship God with praise and joy

To humble ourselves before His throne

and give to God

the highest honour, respect and glory

Always.

Make God your treasure

Your Miracle Is About to Begin

When God wanted a woman to give birth to His son

He didn't choose a prominent girl

but God found favour in an ordinary woman called Mary.

When God needed a new king for Israel

He could have chosen someone distinguished

but God chose an ordinary shepherd boy called David.

When Jesus chose His 12 disciples

He didn't choose men who were well educated

but Jesus took ordinary men willing to follow Him.

God takes ordinary people and performs mighty miracles

All you have to do is love God with all your heart

Give God abundant praise and appreciation

and very soon you will see your miracle begin.

Walking in the Power of God

The Bible is the only book
where the Author is present every time we read it!
Faith is like electricity...it is there all the time
and its force and power work!
When you pray, God sends angels.
Get out of begging and into the praising position.
You need God's Word every day to feed you.
Every breath is a miracle.
Be thankful for each day God gives you.
Don't miss the many opportunities you have
to lay up for yourself treasures in heaven.
Keep your eyes on God's power
and your heart on His love.
God searches our hearts
to see just how much we really love Him!
Remember...God's mighty power
is only a prayer away!

Secrets of Success

You are the architect of your life

Create your own opportunities

and make things happen.

Set yourself a specific goal

and monitor your progress.

Be of service
Keep doing things for others

without counting the cost.

Turn your defeats into victories
Control your environment.

Mix with the kind of

people who inspire you.

Keep your attitude positive

and your health in fine trim.

Let God go before you

in everything you do.

Pray regularly with feeling.

Always be planning

something constantly.

You are the magnet of

your circumstances.

Never give up!

Take the bull by the horns and apply the principles I have shared with you in this book and success will be yours!

THE SECRETS OF LIFE

By BERNARD LEVINE

LOOK FOR THE BEAUTY IN EVERYTHING YOU SEE.
WALK IN PEACE SHOWING KINDNESS
EVERYWHERE.
THE SECRETS OF SUCCESS ARE MOTIVATION
AND DEDICATION.
HAPPINESS IS WHAT YOU MAKE HAPPEN FOR
YOURSELF.
CARING IS GOING TO THE ENDS OF THE WORLD
FOR A STRANGER.
BE USEFUL WITH YOUR LIFE.
WHATEVER YOU ARE DOING PUT YOUR WHOLE
BEING INTO IT 100%.
LOVING IS PLEASING YOUR LOVED ONE EVERYDAY
IN A 1000 DIFFERENT WAYS.
CONTROL YOUR MIND - YOU ARE ITS MASTER - BE
IN CONTROL.
LIVE YOUR LIFE WITHOUT HURTING OR
DESTROYING.
BELIEVE IN YOURSELF. HAVE RESPECT FOR
YOURSELF.
WALK THROUGH LIFE ALWAYS WITH A SONG.

SECRETS OF HAPPINESS

By BERNARD LEVINE

KINDNESS IS THE MOST BEAUTIFUL JEWEL IN THE WORLD.

LOVE MEANS HAVING CONSIDERATION FOR EACH OTHER.

THE SEEDS YOU SOW TODAY WILL BE YOUR FRUIT OF TOMORROW.

FILL YOUR DAY WITH PRAYER AND YOUR LIFE WITH BLESSINGS.

HAPPINESS IS CONTENTMENT FROM WITHIN.

FIND A DREAM TO FOLLOW THAT WILL STIMULATE YOUR MIND.

MAKE LAUGHTER YOUR PARTNER THROUGH LIFE.

BE PREPARED TO FIGHT FOR WHAT YOU WANT OR BELIEVE IN.

A BURNING DESIRE AND SELF-CONFIDENCE ARE THE MAIN SECRETS OF SUCCESS.

REMEMBER - EVERY DAY IS A NEW BEGINNING.

SECRETS OF SUCCESS
By BERNARD LEVINE

You are the architect of your life.
Create your own opportunities and
make things happen.
Set yourself a specific goal
and monitor your progress.
Be of service.
Keep doing things for others
without counting the cost.
Turn your defeats into victories.
Control your environment.
Mix with the kind of
people who inspire you.
Keep your attitude positive
and your health in fine trim.
Let God go before you
in everything you do.
Pray regularly with feeling.
Always be planning something
constantly.
You are the magnet of
your circumstances.
Never give up!

www.ingramcontent.com/pod-product-compliance
Lightning Source LLC
Chambersburg PA
CBHW071827200526
45169CB00018B/1079